NO GREATER LOVE

A Journey through Alzheimer's

Marcia J. Jones

A short story to bring encouragement, comfort, and hope to families in crisis. The message is, "Don't give up!"

Copyright © 2010 by Marcia J. Jones

NO GREATER LOVE
by Marcia J. Jones

Printed in the United States of America

ISBN 9781615798667

All rights reserved solely by the author. The author guarantees all contents are original and do not infringe upon the legal rights of any other person or work. No part of this book may be reproduced in any form without the permission of the author. The views expressed in this book are not necessarily those of the publisher.

Unless otherwise indicated, Bible quotations are taken from *The Living Bible Paraphrased,* Copyright © 1971 by Tyndale House Publishers, Wheaton, Illinois 60187.

www.xulonpress.com

To my dad, James Kirby Malone (1903–1966)

He was my hero and protector. He taught me to trust in Jesus, and I will be eternally grateful for his example.

To my mother, Martha Frances Malone (1916–2002)

She was a tower of strength who overcame difficult situations in her life and displayed loyalty towards my father in his sickness. In addition to all that, she supported four children.

To my grandchildren, Amanda, Emily, Benjamin, Erin, Christopher, and Katelyn

They are the light of my life.

Acknowledgments

Dan Betzer, Pastor—Thank you for being a great man of God. You have preached new life into my soul. I have only been in First Assembly for a short time, but your love for God and your congregation is so obvious. It's a joy to be in your church, and I am glad you are my pastor.

Brenda Pitts, Author—Thank you for the wonderful job you did with your professional critique and editing of this book. You felt my heart, and you were a real blessing to me.

Karla LaFreniere—You went beyond the call of duty and extended kindness and compassion to Jimmy when he resided at Arden Courts.

Dr. Bill Beckwith, PhD—Thank you for being Jimmy's advocate and my friend during his illness and death.

Thank you to my family and friends who gave unwavering support to me. James and Paul, you made me proud with the loving tributes you wrote for Jimmy's memorial service.

IN MEMORY OF

James Harold Jones

James W. Krewson, Sr.

Thelma (Mom) Krewson

My forever friend, Kathy Aldrich Hall

Endorsements

My husband and I pastored at Full Gospel Tabernacle (now Grace Church) in East St. Louis, Illinois, and I watched Marcia and Jim (Jimmy) grow up from early childhood. Jim's father was on our Deacon board. Marcia's father was very faithful to bring all his children to church every Sunday and raised them to know God in a personal way. He believed Proverbs 22:6 that says "Train up a child in the way he should go, and when he is old, he will not depart from it." I have watched Marcia, her sister and brothers become mature Christians as a result of their father's prayers. Their families now are also serving God.

"No Greater Love" is truly a love story that will encourage anyone who has a loved one with Alzheimer's disease, or who is a caregiver, to understand the true meaning of love. You will laugh as well as weep with Marcia as you read about how she "didn't give up" during her time of crisis.

Helen Redman, Director
Christian Missionary Association,
Skiatook, Oklahoma

"No Greater Love" tells life as it really is…real hurt, real pain, real love, real joy, real heartbreak, real peace...real life! You will be touched and challenged as you experience "No Greater Love."

Hal F. Santos, Lead Pastor - Grace Church,
Fairview Heights, Illinois

Contents

Thoughts About Jim Jones xv

Introduction xvii

Chapter 1   Chaos! 21

Chapter 2   The Terrible Teens 34

Chapter 3   Jumping from the Frying Pan into the Fire 41

Chapter 4   A Gift from the Past 49

Chapter 5   Time with Mama 62

Chapter 6   Let Freedom Ring! 68

Chapter 7   The Transition 76

Chapter 8   The Grand Finale 84

Chapter 9	What Do I Do Now?	91
Conclusion		95
Epilogue		97
Thoughts About Grief		99
A New Beginning		103
Tips for Caregivers, Friends, and Families		105
Old Couple Walks the Beach		109

Thoughts about Jim Jones

I first met Jim (Jimmy) Jones when he was in the early stages of Alzheimer's disease. Little did I know at the time that we would develop a deep and growing relationship. As Jim's disease progressed, our friendship grew and flourished. Jim had been a very good athlete and continued to love sports and his St. Louis Cardinals. He also loved the outdoors. Many of our visits were spent taking walks outside while enjoying God's creation and talking sports. During one Christmas holiday we sat outside in a gazebo and sang Christmas carols.

Jim Jones was a man's man who was serious about his relationship with his God. Jim taught me that it is okay to cry out to our heavenly Father and leave everything in His hands. I was Jim's pastor and I looked forward to our visits. But even more than this, I was Jim's friend and his brother in Christ. I am thankful for what Jim taught me and for the time we shared together.

Dr. Vaughn Stanley, PhD
Fort Myers, Florida

Introduction

After I retired at the age of fifty-seven, my life began to unravel. In spite of the many problems I had faced throughout my life, I had always been able to hold things together. I was a social worker, counselor, singles' and youth minister, and birthright counselor. I served on various community boards, and I was proud that I had control of my life. After taking care of my mother when she had Alzheimer's, I patted myself on the back at what a good daughter I was in spite of the abuse she had inflicted on me as a child. When she died, I thought I would finally have time for myself.

My husband and I retired six months after my mother's death with big plans to have fun traveling, fishing, and cruising. During the first week of retirement, I noticed my husband was having memory issues. I took him to our internist, who said, "He is too young to have Alzheimer's. He is just having retirement issues." However, I insisted on an MRI for my husband and a referral to a neurologist. Months later, my husband was diagnosed with early-onset Alzheimer's. This was not in our plans. We were both only fifty-seven and this was supposed to be our time of life.

When my mother became ill with Alzheimer's and I became her caregiver, I decided I would write a book about my experience. Little did I know then that God had more chapters to add to my story. Originally, I had planned to write about my life as an abused child and what it was like to care for the one who had abused me. I felt I had overcome the environment I had grown up in. After all, I had worked for seventeen years as a state social worker involved in child abuse investigations, foster care, and adoptions. I did not physically abuse my children, and I tried to be a good parent. I was filled with pride.

During the years of my mother's illness, I experienced much anxiety but pushed it aside and stepped into the role of devoted daughter. Now, with my husband's diagnosis, I would be assuming the role of devoted wife. My life seemed to be falling apart around me, and I felt myself losing control. A storm was raging inside. Having had no time to recover from taking care of my mother, I was to be a caregiver once more. I couldn't help thinking it wasn't fair, no matter how much I loved my husband.

In the ensuing years, I adjusted to the many changes in my husband and managed our life together. Despite the fact that he had received the same diagnosis as did my mother, the caregiving experience was different this time. But all throughout, God met my needs repeatedly and worked many little miracles along the way.

When you are finished reading this book, I pray you will find hope, comfort, and the knowledge that you can lean on God no matter where life has taken you. No matter what your situation may be, God is there, and He loves you. There is *no greater love*, and I pray you will discover that.

Chapter 1

Chaos!

I remember the moment as though it were yesterday. I was sitting on a pony having my picture made in front of our three-room flat on Twenty-Fifth Street in East St. Louis, Illinois. I was four years old, and I was a happy little girl. If only life could have stayed that simple for our family.

By the time I started grade school, however, I was more aware of my parents' problems. They fought constantly. My mother was very unhappy and had been a victim of alcoholism and poverty while growing up. When she was in her seventies, she was finally able to share her painful life story with me. We created a wonderful relationship, and I tutored her every Saturday as she studied her catechism to join St. John's Lutheran Church in St. Louis, Missouri. But while I was growing up, my mother inflicted much emotional pain upon me by abusing me. I don't think she did it intentionally; she just didn't know how to cope with the hardships she had experienced in her life.

The first time I remember my mother losing control was when I was five years old. My mother screamed at my father about our finances and then hit him with a lamp. He responded by taking off his shoe and hitting her in the leg. Lying in my little rollaway bed in a bedroom that looked like a hallway, I put my head under the covers and tried to ignore what was happening. Incidents like this occurred from time to time, but even when things were not quite so volatile, there was constant yelling in our home.

We were a family of six living in that small three-room flat. My two brothers slept in the same tiny room as did I, and they provided the security I needed to not feel alone when fighting erupted between my parents at bedtime. My sister stayed in a crib in my parents' bedroom.

Despite the yelling and sometimes violent outbursts, some of the best times of my life took place in that apartment where I lived until I was eight years old. Daddy and I would sometimes walk to Johnny's Doughnut Shop, which was a mile from our home. About two blocks from Johnny's, we could already smell the doughnuts as we walked down the sidewalk towards the shop. To this day, whenever I walk through a bakery department or into a doughnut shop, I remember those times.

Another fun thing Daddy and I did was to walk seven blocks to Velvet Freeze for ice cream. On Sunday nights, I usually went to church with my dad, and we would go to Velvet Freeze beforehand as part of our routine. It seems like only yesterday, and it's hard to believe all those years have passed.

As the years rolled by, we eventually moved to a rental home with two bedrooms. My little sister and I slept on a rollaway bed in the living room. The fighting between my parents was ongoing, and my mother's bitterness was growing. One day when I was thirteen, I was sitting at the kitchen table while my mother ironed our clothes. My father walked into the room, and my mother looked at him and said, "I will spit on your grave when you die!"

My dad walked over to her and grabbed her, and my mother yelled, "Marcia, help me. Please help me!"

Reacting in panic, I got out of my chair and grabbed a rolling pin and hit my father in the shoulder. He released his grip on my mother and turned to me and asked, "What did I ever do to you to deserve that?"

"Nothing," I meekly answered. Then I started crying and left the kitchen. Later when I was alone, I cried my eyes out. I loved my father with all my heart and I wondered if he would ever forgive me.

My dad was not an affectionate person, but later that day when he said, "Marcia, you want to play checkers?" I knew he still loved me and forgave me. I was so relieved. I have asked myself through the years why I hit my father, my protector, and there is no good answer. I just felt scared and didn't think about what I was doing. I was a child, and I just wanted the fighting to stop between my mother and father.

A few months later, Daddy and I went shopping for a birthday gift for my mother. As we rode the bus home, Daddy asked, "Do you think Mama will like the watch I bought for her?"

I smiled and said, "Yes, Daddy, Mama will love it." We were both so excited about giving it to her.

When we got home, my father wrapped the watch and presented it to Mama while she was sitting at the kitchen table drinking coffee. Daddy said, "Happy birthday, Martha." She opened the box, took the watch out, and walked over to the wastebasket and threw it into the trash.

I thought to myself, *Oh God, please don't let her yell at Daddy*. To my relief, she said nothing and just went back to reading her magazine. Daddy said nothing either. He walked out of the room, and I went to him and put my arm around his waist, not saying a word. We got out the checkerboard and played.

Another example of my mother's dysfunctional behavior was the way she handled a crisis in my life when I was ten years old. My Aunt Dessie and her boyfriend, Tom, invited me to take a trip with them to southern Missouri and Olathe, Kansas. My aunt had met Tom at a tent revival. He was becoming a welcome visitor in our house and brought religious tracts to my father. Overall, Tom seemed like a nice guy, and everyone was happy that my spinster aunt was dating someone.

I was very excited about the trip. Since our family did not own a car, I had never been on a trip farther than twenty-five miles from home. We were traveling from East St. Louis, Illinois, to Olathe, Kansas, where my Aunt Ruth and Uncle Howard lived. I couldn't wait to spend a week with my cousin Carol.

NO GREATER LOVE

When we arrived at our relatives' home, Aunt Dessie said she and Tom were going to Summersville, Missouri, to visit relatives and would be back the following week to pick me up. Five days later, Tom showed up in Kansas and said, "Martha called and wants me to bring Marcia home." He said Aunt Dessie had decided to stay a few weeks longer in Summersville. Everyone trusted Tom—they had no reason not to.

On our trip home, we stopped at a fireworks stand in Missouri. Tom said, "Do you like firecrackers?"

I smiled and answered, "I love to shoot firecrackers!"

Tom replied, "How about I buy you all the fireworks you want for the Fourth of July?"

I got a basket and started filling it up with sparklers, firecrackers, cherry bombs, bottle rockets, bulldogs, flares, and caps. It felt like Christmas! As we drove on towards Dexter, Missouri, Tom made a statement that I did not understand. He said, "Now when we get to my sister's house tonight, you can sleep with me."

I nodded my head and shyly responded, "Okay." I wondered why he wanted me to sleep with him.

We soon stopped for lunch and then hit the road again. We were now driving in the country with nothing but woods around us. Tom pulled the car over to the side of the road, and I asked, "Why are we stopping here?"

He replied evasively, "Oh, we'll just rest for a little bit." Tom then turned his head to look at me and said, "You know, I used to touch your cousin Amy [not her real name]. Let me show you what I did to her." Aunt Dessie and Tom had visited my cousin's house many times, and now I was feeling scared thinking of what he could have done to Amy. As Tom started to unbutton my blouse, I felt fearful of what he might do to me.

All of a sudden from out of nowhere on that lonely old abandoned road, a highway patrol car showed up. The officer got out of his vehicle and walked over to our car and asked, "Is there a problem?"

Tom quickly answered, "No problem, officer. I'm her uncle, and we were just taking a rest."

Somehow I had the presence of mind to protest, "He's not my uncle," and I jumped out of the car. The next thing I did was to run over to the uniformed officer and hug him as tightly as I could. The officer called for backup, and another patrol car soon arrived and took Tom away in handcuffs. I rode back to the tiny satellite station with the patrol officer and ate a hamburger and French fries, which I downed with a strawberry malt. I don't remember where the officer got the food, but I gobbled it up. He told me he had contacted my parents, and I would be going home on a bus in a few hours.

Later that night around ten, I arrived at the Greyhound bus station in St. Louis. Since we did not own a car, our neighbors, Frank and Ann, met me at the bus depot. They gave me a hug and then took me home.

As soon as I entered our house, my mother shut the door behind me and started yelling. She screamed, "Tell me what that man did to you!" Then she stormed over to my father and sneered, "If you were a real man, you would go out and kill him."

My dad responded sarcastically, "I'm sure that would make things all better, woman."

I ran into the bathroom, sobbing. I finally made myself throw up, as though throwing up would empty out all the pain inside of me. It didn't. Broken, I thought my mother was blaming me for Tom's attempt to molest me.

All evening my mother ranted about how evil men were. But after that, we never talked about it again. Two months later, my parents received a call from the court that Tom had pled guilty and was being sent to prison. I would not have to testify. During the course of the investigation, the police had also discovered that Tom had a wife and children in California. My aunt was devastated, and my father decided that maybe not everyone who claimed to be a Christian really was. He called Tom a "wolf in sheep's clothing."

Another traumatic experience occurred one summer when I was in junior high. I was playing in a band concert in a park on the other side of town, and because we did not own a car, my mother had to take me on a bus. To reach the park, we had to transfer buses, and my mother's anger began to escalate as a result of the inconvenience. With a fierce look on her face, she announced, "I've worked hard all day, and this makes me mad." I silently prayed, *Please, God, don't let my mother get angry.*

But Mama's wrath raged unabated even after we arrived at the park. As we walked towards the bandstand, she glared at me and said, "I'm going to kill you."

I was frantic. I spotted a police officer and desperately declared, "Mama, I'm going to tell that policeman over there!"

That seemed to jolt her back into reality. She started crying and took me into a restroom and sobbed, "Marcia, I'm sorry. I'm just so tired from working all day. Please don't tell the policeman. I didn't mean it."

Minutes after this disturbing exchange, I played my clarinet in the band and wondered what I had done wrong. I asked myself, *Why does Mama hate me so much?* There were other band concerts throughout the years, but I remember only my father in attendance at those.

When I was twelve years old, my father suffered a massive heart attack. That day is still very vivid in my mind, emblazoned on my memory. Daddy looked tired that morning, and I remember him being sort of slumped over as he got ready for his three-mile walk to work, lunch pail in hand. He told Mama he didn't feel good but would go to work anyway because we needed the money. Later that summer morning, the doctor's office called my mother and told her Daddy was being taken to the hospital and was very ill. Our lives changed forever with that phone call.

Daddy did not look the same when he came home from the hospital. Our neighbor's car pulled up to our house, and when Daddy got out, I noticed right away that his black hair was now gray. I felt a little frightened when I saw him. I thought, *Is this old man my father?*

Daddy's sickness made Mama even meaner because it placed more responsibility on her. In addition to her cleaning people's houses and ironing clothes, she had to find a job, since Daddy was not allowed to return to his factory job. The company doctor told him he would be dead in six months, but he lived for another thirteen years.

During that time, Daddy became "Mr. Mom" in our household. All of a sudden, he was in charge of four kids. I suspect this may have been more challenging for him than working in a factory! He had to become chef and housekeeper. But Daddy rose to the challenge and became a very good cook, and I fondly remember pulling taffy with him.

With the change in our household, Mama seemed like she hated Daddy and me more than ever. At the time, I did not understand her bitterness, but as I grew older, I realized the tremendous stress she was under. When I was helping my seventy-five-year-old mother study her catechism for joining the Lutheran Church, Mama gave me a glimpse into what her world had been like in those trying days.

Mama told me that one year when she was working at the biscuit company after my father had to retire, she was laid off in the middle of December. When they informed her of her job loss, Mama was desperate because she had no money to purchase Christmas gifts for any of her children. She told me she went to the second floor of the building and was going to jump out the bathroom window and kill herself. Thankfully, a supervisor came into the bathroom and told Mama he would take her home and that everything would get better.

That evening Mama cried to my father, "Daddy, I don't know what we are going to do. The kids must have a good Christmas."

Daddy soothingly replied, "Martha, the Lord will take care of us, and the kids will have a good Christmas." The very next day, Mama's supervisor came over with money collected for our family from Mama's coworkers. It was two hundred dollars, which was a lot of money back in the late fifties. Needless to say, we had a great Christmas.

Despite my father's physical limitations, it took him years to be approved for disability through Social Security. When Daddy finally received a check for all those years of disability, he and I took a bus downtown to pay off our debts to our doctor and two pharmacies. During those years, our doctor had continued treating our entire family without demanding payment. He just kept a running tab. The two pharmacies where we got our medicines also gave us credit during those years, well knowing it might be a long time before they were paid. Daddy breathed a huge sigh of relief when he paid off the medical bills and was finally out of debt.

When I was fourteen, Mama choked on a chicken bone that became lodged in her windpipe. The first attempt to remove the bone did not work, so the doctor brought in a specialist who finally removed it. Mama was in the hospital for two months and almost died because of complications.

NO GREATER LOVE

I remember visiting Mama while she was in the hospital, walking a few miles daily from Rock Junior High to St. Mary's Hospital in East St. Louis. Mama would often say, "Marcia Jean, hold on to me so I can walk." These walks usually ended up with Mama feeling faint. That always scared me because I was afraid she would fall before I could get her back to bed. However, Mama was a determined woman and had so much grit. She never gave up. Mama was so strong.

My mother finally left the hospital one week before Christmas. She insisted on going shopping, and we did just that on a very snowy day. Mama still had a sense of humor in spite of the feeling that life had let her down. We were walking along the sidewalk in front of a department store when a woman slipped and fell on the ice. Mama got hysterical with laughter, and then I started cackling like a hen. Pretty soon the lady on the sidewalk was in stitches, too! I helped her up while Mama continued to laugh uncontrollably. I was so embarrassed, but I was still laughing as I helped the lady up. We all said "Merry Christmas," and the lady went on her way. Mama and I looked at each other, and we were soon roaring with laughter again. What a wonderful memory that is to remember Mama laughing after almost dying in the hospital!

For Mama, Christmas was always special, and she wanted my siblings and me to enjoy the holiday. Mama said her father, who died shortly after she and my father were married, had been an alcoholic. One Christmas, in a drunken stupor, he had knocked over their Christmas tree. She wanted better for her children.

Mama said her childhood was tough because her family was so poor. Children at school often made fun of her sackcloth clothing. Mama always said Grandma was a saint and that Grandpa was wonderful when he didn't drink. She called him "Pop" and remembered him as a very loving man.

In 1993 on Good Friday, I received a call from my aging mother. Mama was crying. Alarmed, I asked, "Mama, what is wrong?"

Between sobs, my mother got out, "You don't know what happened to me."

As a social worker, my antennae immediately went up. I gently asked, "Mama, did your father touch you?"

"No, but someone else did," she sobbed. She then proceeded to tell me that she had been raped by an adult male relative when she was only eight years old. He had threatened to kill her parents if she told. She confessed she had never felt good about herself after this incident. Mama said she could not concentrate in class after the rape and struggled with her schoolwork, eventually dropping out of high school at age sixteen. The horrible abuse completely changed the direction of her life.

Hearing this heartbreaking story and knowing Mama had lived with this all those years filled my heart with compassion. I think Mama felt safe talking to me, and it marked a real breakthrough in our relationship. From that point on, she began telling me how much she had always loved me, and she seemed to experience genuine remorse for having hurt me. What a burden Mama had carried all her life!

With Mama's confession, I could no longer feel anger over the abuse she had perpetrated against me. I put myself in her shoes and asked myself how I would have felt if a relative or anyone else had done that to me. Mama carried a lifelong secret, an unhealed wound, that affected her even into adulthood. It influenced every aspect of her behavior in every area of her life.

One of the things my sons remember most about their grandmother was the terrible fear that dominated her. When she visited our home in Hannibal, Missouri, she would double-check the locks on our doors and would pull down all the shades on the windows. If my sons went out to shoot baskets in the driveway, she would go out and watch every move they made. She would go walking with one of my sons and then come home crying, unable to tell us what was troubling her. None of it made any sense at the time, but later, after I learned her terrible secret, I understood. I could no longer be mad at my mama.

Chapter 2

The Terrible Teens

When I started high school in 1960, I appeared to be just a normal teenager to everyone. On the outside, I was happy and had friends. However, on the inside, I experienced much anxiety. I remember going to our family doctor for stomach problems when I was fifteen. He asked me to put my hands out in front of my body. When I did, they shook. Curious, he asked, "Why are you so nervous and shaky?"

I answered matter-of-factly, "My mother hits me with her fists and belts and calls me names. It scares me." It felt so good to finally tell someone.

My doctor was uncomfortable with my response and brushed it away, saying, "You will be fine." He took it no further, and we never mentioned it again. This experience taught me to keep my mouth shut.

My mother's physical abuse of me started when I was a high school sophomore. If I sent my boyfriend home too early, Mama would become enraged and

NO GREATER LOVE

beat me. I had homework to do, but this meant nothing to her. My boyfriend lived next door to me, and he later told me that he would hear me screaming after he went home. He said he thought it was my little sister getting a whipping.

Mama became very upset if I did not have a date on weekends. One Friday night, my best friend, Kathy, was spending the night. My mother asked us both, "Why aren't you girls out on dates?"

When we were alone later, Kathy remarked, puzzled, "I don't understand. My mother would be thrilled if we were with her on a weekend night." But not Mama. Mama constantly told me I was going to be an old maid. She compared me to my cousins or neighbors, and I was never good enough for her.

Mama wanted me to be popular. I had to go to every dance in high school. If I didn't, I knew another beating would result. Consequently, I didn't miss a dance, even if I had to ask the guy! I think Mama was trying to live her life through me. She had been denied so many things in life, and she loved seeing me in my formals. She always took pictures and was very happy on prom nights.

Another reason for my mother's abuse towards me was my love for God and church. Throughout the years, Mama had hardened her heart towards the church and God, and she showed no mercy towards me concerning my interest in spiritual things. One night as I was on my way out the door to attend church, Mama drew back her fists and shouted, "You no-good holy roller. You're just like your father!" She then lunged at me and shoved me against the door, breaking the glass and causing me to cut my hand. Mama stood there cursing at me as I walked down the sidewalk, crying. When I got to church, my pastor, Henry Redman, took me into his office and treated the cut on my hand.

Later, when I decided I wanted to go to Bible college to become a missionary, Mama threatened, "If you go, you will never see your little sister again. I'll make sure of that!" Out of fear of never seeing Cheryl again, I did not pursue the ministry.

One of Mama's favorite forms of abuse was to corner me in the bathroom where I couldn't escape and knock me into the tub and beat me with her fists. She also liked to use the buckle end of a belt to draw blood. I often went to school with welts, scratches, or cuts on my arms and legs. Amazingly, no teacher ever asked me about them; I suppose that was because child abuse was basically ignored back in the early sixties. Some of the kids in my gym class did ask questions, but my best friend, Kathy, always came up with a clever story. I could always count on her to protect me.

Mama possessed the same hatred for Daddy as she had for me. She once threw him across the dining room when he tried to keep her from hitting me. He did his best to protect me and even put a lock on my bedroom door to keep Mama out, but Mama was too strong for the lock. She broke it down and came after me.

I once asked Mama why she hated Daddy and me, and she spewed, "You are both holy rollers." One time she jumped right into my father's face and called him that—a holy roller. Unperturbed, he told her it was a good thing he was a holy roller or he would have knocked her down. I tried hard not to smile at this exchange, but I was so glad he had stood up to her. That did not happen very often, though. Like the rest of us, Daddy was afraid of her.

If Mama could have accepted our love, it would have made life easier for all of us. But that was not to be at this time. I truly believe Daddy did the very best he could to protect me from Mama's unrelenting anger and abuse, but it just wasn't enough. When I turned eighteen, I informed Mama that if she ever laid a hand on me again, I would leave. Two weeks later, she came at me, beating me with her fists, and true to my word, I left. That began a pattern that continued for the next two years.

During those times, I would move out, go back home a little later, only to move out again. I rented three different apartments in two years. Each time I moved out, I hated leaving my little sister behind because we had always shared a bedroom from the time she was out of her crib. I was seven years older than Cheryl, and I felt protective towards her, but I just couldn't stay in that abusive environment.

I finally moved in with my friend Louise Hrasky and her family. Louise was one of my friends from high school, and she had once told me I could live with her if my mother tried to hurt me again. One Sunday night, I arrived home from church, and Mama took a swing at me as I was walking to my room. I showed up at Louise's that night, and Ann, her mother, opened her arms and heart to me. That began a special time in my life. I was part of a family

NO GREATER LOVE

that showed me love, and I was safe. They treated me as though I belonged.

I lived there six months until Uncle Woody, my dad's brother, died unexpectedly in a car wreck. I felt I should go home and be with Daddy, so that is what I did. The day my uncle died, was the only time I ever saw Daddy cry. A single tear rolled out of his eye as I hugged him, but he quickly wiped it away.

When I was nineteen years of age, I needed surgery to remove a grapefruit-sized ovarian cyst. I had never been to a gynecologist, and I was so scared of the exam. The doctor was appalled that my mother was not with me. As he was examining me, he asked, "Why isn't your mother with you for your first exam?" Teary-eyed, I told him about my mother's abuse. He was very compassionate, but I could tell by his demeanor that he was very angry about what had happened to me.

After the surgery, I was rolled out of the operating room, and my mother approached the doctor to ask about my condition. The doctor answered her abruptly, "Your daughter is an adult. You will have to get any medical information from her." That infuriated Mama.

When I awoke in my room, my mother was standing over me, fists drawn and yelling and cursing. I immediately went into shock, and the hospital personnel forced her to leave. I was given a large dose of morphine, and I slept for twenty-four hours.

Performed in the sixties, the operation was quite extensive. My entire abdomen had to be cut open, and they removed not only my ovary but also my appendix. When I was discharged from the hospital, I was still looking at five more weeks of recovery before I could return to work.

When I arrived home after leaving the hospital, my mother went on a rampage. She began yelling at me, telling me I was weak and sickly like my father. I could barely walk and just wanted to go to bed, but Mama continued her tirade. So I called Will Rosene, one of my bosses from work, and his wife, Bernice, picked me up and took me to their summer home and nursed me back to health. I was so grateful that God provided me with two very kind people to love and pray for me during my healing time.

I hated leaving Daddy and Cheryl, but they were powerless to stop my mother's physical abuse against me. I called home almost daily while Mama was at work to make sure Daddy was okay. As soon as I was able to return to work, I moved back home. In the back of my mind, I feared for Daddy and Cheryl's safety because they were the two people who attempted to physically protect me.

Cheryl was seven years younger than me, but she stood up for me the best she could. As I have said, the abuse started when I was fifteen, and I remember my eight-year-old-sister jumping in front of me and daring to tell our mother, "Don't hurt my sissy! Don't hurt my sissy!" That memory still brings tears to my eyes. My sister and I shared the same bed and went to sleep holding hands the entire time I lived at home, so our bond was close and strong.

My brother Jim was already grown and was usually working when Mom's fury raged. He was somewhat shocked and saddened when I told him about the abuse. Jim asked me a few years ago, "Marsh, do you remember when Mom just hated the world?" Oh yes, I remember it well.

My brother Jerry, who was two years younger than me, usually ran to his room when trouble erupted. I didn't blame him; it was scary living in our home. I remember one time I went flying up the steps to his room while Mama was chasing after me and hitting me with her fists, and he was just sitting on his bed looking so scared. It was crazy times for the Malone family. No one remained untouched by my mother's dysfunction.

Chapter 3

Jumping from the Frying Pan into the Fire

I met my first husband, Jim K., at work. We spent a lot of time together on the job, and one day he asked if he could take me home after work. Driving me home, he sweetly confessed, "I think I'm falling in love with you." Jim asked me to have dinner with him and his mother the coming weekend. I accepted, and when I was introduced to his mother, she immediately said, "Oh, just call me Mom." That was it for me. I finally had a mother who approved of me. From that day on, Jim's mother became a surrogate mother to me. We loved each other until the day she died. In my heart, she was "Mom."

The ironic part about my relationship with Jim was that my mother loved him. He was everything physically that my father was not. Jim was a big, husky guy, and Mama would say, "Now that's what I call a real man!" This statement was especially degrading to my dad and brothers because of the way she said it and because my dad and brothers were thin.

I think my mother loved Jim in an unhealthy way. He gave her the attention that she craved from my father. My mother did not think Jim could do any wrong. Because of her attraction to Jim, I was now worthy of her approval, and she quit beating me.

Jim and I were married a few years later. On our wedding day, he promised me that he would never let my mother hit me again. And although my mother never laid a hand on me after Jim came into my life, I still feared her. Some wounds heal slowly—if at all.

Jim and I moved from Illinois to California. We had been there only a short time when I decided to call my dad on my coffee break at my job one day. I just felt like I needed to talk to him. I dialed the number apprehensively, and when Daddy answered, I blurted out, "Daddy, are you okay?"

Daddy answered straightforwardly, "Marcia, I passed out a few nights ago. Didn't your mother tell you?" I told him that no, Mama hadn't called me.

Later that night I said to Jim, "Honey, I'm worried about Daddy. Do you think we could handle it financially for me to fly back home?" The trip would mean that Jim and I would be apart on Thanksgiving, since we couldn't afford for both of us to go.

But Jim understood and urged me to go. "Hon," he explained, "you cannot afford not to go. You have my blessing, and I think you should go. I will be fine."

I called Mama to tell her I would be coming in for Thanksgiving. Her comment was, "What will people think of you coming by yourself? It won't look right."

"Mama," I responded firmly, "I am coming home, and I am coming alone." I didn't care what others thought. Daddy needed me—that was all that mattered.

Mama wasn't happy about my decision, but I flew home anyway. I felt very strongly that I should spend time with Daddy. During that brief four-day visit, I spent some time alone with my father. One day we were sitting on the couch looking at pictures, and he asked me, "Marcia, are you happy with Jim?" I assured him I was indeed happy. Daddy added, almost as an afterthought, "Well, I just needed to know you were happy."

That visit was the last time I saw my father alive. In the years following, I often thought how glad I was that I had not let my mother intimidate me into staying in California. I would have missed that one last visit with my beloved daddy. Two days after I returned to California, my father had a massive heart attack and died. My anchor was gone. I just couldn't believe it—I didn't want to believe it—but it was true.

Soon after returning to Los Angeles, I learned I was pregnant with my first son, James. Knowing I was carrying a new life in my body helped ease the loss of my dad. I quit my job shortly into the pregnancy, and Jim and I rented an apartment in Hollywood, California. That first Christmas, Jim and I had no extra money to buy gifts for each other. But when I woke up on Christmas morning, I found a big, pink stuffed poodle under the tree, with a card on it

NO GREATER LOVE

that read, "Love, Santa." Jim had gone down to the gas station around the corner while I was sleeping and bought it for me. He knew I still loved stuffed animals, even though I was a grown woman.

As the days of my pregnancy increased, so did Jim's drinking. I had grown up in a household with no alcohol and no ashtrays. I was very naïve, and I did not understand what an alcoholic was. Sadly, I soon learned. Many years later, I learned from Jim's mother that Jim had a problem even when we were dating. After he would drop me off at my house, he would return home to their apartment and drink.

As Jim's alcoholism progressed, our fighting increased. We both had brought baggage into this marriage, and at times it was overwhelming. From time to time, Jim turned violent, and I was thrust back into the environment of my childhood. What I didn't realize then was that Jim had many years of drinking under his belt before I ever met him. He later told me that he had blackouts long before he even knew me. Jim said that during the fifties, he would fly from St. Louis to New Jersey, hold a meeting, and fly back home again, all while in an alcoholic blackout. Now, in these early years of our marriage, he had progressed to the point where he could not control his drinking.

As Jim's drinking increased, the violence heightened. James and I would hide in a bathroom and lock the door when Jim drank too much and threatened us. Sometimes we ran to a neighbor's home. I had no relatives close by. Jim was a good man when he wasn't drinking. He had a PhD in architecture and had a very high IQ, but he lost many jobs because of his alcoholism.

There is, however, a silver lining in this story. In 1974, Jim took a job away from home with the intent that James, Paul, and I would join him later. Three days after he started his new high-paying job with a major oil company, he failed to show up for work. I called Pastor Redman and asked if he knew someone in the Richmond, Virginia, area who could go over to Jim's apartment to see if he was okay. Pastor Redman made some calls and found a minister in the area.

The minister, John, went to Jim's apartment on a Sunday afternoon and found him drunk, unkempt, and a total mess. He told Jim he needed God, and Jim acknowledged that he did. They prayed together, and Jim said the sinner's prayer. Jim went to church with John that evening and made his way to the altar to pray again.

After the service, John took Jim home with him, telling him he thought it best for Jim to sleep at his house. Jim was afraid he would experience the DTs (delirium tremors) as he had in the past. John's mother-in-law lived with him, and she told Jim he would not have them because God had healed him. However, she assured him she would sit in a chair next to his bed, if that would allow him to sleep. Before Jim went to sleep that night, this little woman of God prayed with him, and there was a lot of crying and repenting. Jim slept like a baby, and the next morning he awoke totally restored by God.

I wish I could say we lived a perfect life after Jim was miraculously saved and healed from alcoholism.

NO GREATER LOVE

But we had already suffered a great deal of damage to our relationship, and back in the seventies, few resources existed to help us restore our marriage. After Jim's conversion, we became very active in church. I taught Sunday school, sang in the choir, and worked in various ministries. Jim and I had a great home for entertaining and often invited couples from the church to our home. However, we desperately needed good Christian counseling, which was nowhere to be found.

As we were struggling with our problems, our church was in the middle of a good old-fashioned church fight. The pastor was distanced from his congregation, and shamefully the people of God were too busy sparring between themselves to minister to Jim and me in our time of need. Jim was experiencing legal problems, our household was in crisis, and we needed love from our church. It didn't happen.

Jim and I divorced in 1984, and it was very hurtful. Despite everything that had happened, we never quit loving each other. It was not a romantic, sexual love that remained, but rather the deep, abiding love of friendship. I never stopped loving my wonderful mother-in-law, either. Jim, his mother, and I remained good friends until they both died.

The breakup of my family is a sadness that has never truly left me, but I hold the good memories within my heart. Jim often told me he worshiped me, and he was totally devoted to me. With Jim, I had the assurance he would never abandon me. To this day, the breakup of our marriage still stings.

NO GREATER LOVE

I had been single for one year when Jim remarried. It broke my heart. Like my father, he had been my protector, when he was sober. I knew the real Jim, the man without the alcohol.

A year later, I met an outgoing photographer named Jake (not his real name) in a restaurant at lunch. Jake seemed so happy and was very pleasant. He asked if he could call me, and I gave him my telephone number. He called later that day at my office where I was a counselor at a women's recovery center. We went on our first date that weekend, and he went to church with me the following weekend.

Everyone who met Jake loved his personality. He was always whistling and had a smile on his face. Before long, he was running the video camera at church. We were married three months from the date we met. That decision would be the worst decision I have ever made in my life.

In the eighteen months we were married, Jake had eight jobs. When he lost a job, he didn't tell me. I would call him at work only to be told he was no longer working there. Jake was also abusive. On the day of our divorce, Jake was in jail for violating a restraining order against me. I later found out from his ex-wife that he had abused her and their son, too. She said when Jake threw their son across the room, that was the final straw for her and she made the decision to divorce him.

Jake's ex-wife also shocked me when she informed me that Jake had a wife before her and a son by that marriage. Jake had not told me any of this. Jake had also said that he was a former Navy

NO GREATER LOVE

SEAL, but his ex-wife said this was not true. These were just a few of Jake's lies.

I had a difficult time forgiving myself for this mistake, but God cleansed my heart and helped me. Jim, the boys' father, also helped me by changing all the locks in my house in case Jake ever tried to come back. Jake got out of jail the day of our divorce and immediately found another woman to support him.

Chapter 4

A Gift from the Past

I had been single for four years when God brought a new Jim into my life to love. This Jim was the little Jimmy Jones I had grown up with in Full Gospel Tabernacle in East St. Louis, Illinois. During our teen years, Jimmy had stood behind me in youth choir.

Jimmy had seen my relatives on three different occasions and asked about me. He called me three different times to ask me out, but it wasn't until the third phone call (four years later!) that I finally agreed to go out with him on a date. I didn't think we would have a thing in common, and I was very apprehensive about going out with him.

My fears, however, were unfounded, as we spent three hours talking at dinner and another two hours talking in the car. I think we told each other our entire lives' stories in one night. Jimmy admitted to me later that when we were growing up, he thought I was a snob, and I confessed to him that I had thought he was a big nerd. We were both so wrong! Being with Jimmy that night, I had an instant feeling of trust, knowing we had grown up in the same church. Jimmy was stable and a straight arrow. He seemed like a man in charge, and I liked that about him.

I dated Jimmy for over a year before we were married. A few years into our marriage, I discovered that Jimmy was full of pain from the blows life had dealt him. He hid it well at first, but as we became closer, he opened up to me about his distrust towards the people he felt had abandoned him in some way.

Jimmy never tried to reconcile with the people who had hurt him. His way of dealing with problems was not to deal with them. He said he wasn't cut out for dealing with "those kinds of things." Unfortunately, he never really resolved these issues before he died. He did, however, have peace about our life together and his relationship with God.

When Jimmy was diagnosed with Alzheimer's, his first question to me was the same he had asked when we decided to marry: would I always be there for him? He wanted assurance that I would never leave him. His painful life experiences had made him feel he couldn't truly rely on anyone. I gave him the same answer that I had given him when he proposed: he could count on me to stay with him forever.

I've never in my entire life felt such a strong commitment to be there for someone and to be as totally immersed in their life as I did with Jimmy. This feeling is what kept me going day after day for five long years. When I placed Jimmy in assisted living, I saw him daily, except when exhaustion would overcome me and I had to take a day off. It was important to me to let him lean on me throughout his terrible illness.

The payoff was huge for me. As unbelievable as it may sound, the greatest night of my life was the night my husband Jimmy died in my arms. Lying with him and holding him in that tiny hospital bed was the ultimate spiritual experience, and never have I felt the presence of God as I did that night. With God's help, I kept my word to Jimmy that I would be there when he died. What a wonderful gift from God!

The only other time I experienced a similar feeling occurred many years after my father had died. He died around Thanksgiving, and yearly I would grow depressed and start missing him around the holidays. Fourteen years after his death, I was praying and pouring my heart out to God. I told Him how much I missed my dad, and I asked Him to tell Daddy hello for me. I then fell asleep and had the most wonderful dream.

In my dream, I saw Daddy standing by a river with Jesus. He looked so wonderful, and his gray hair was now black. He wasn't wearing his glasses, and I realized he didn't need them anymore. Jesus was facing him, and suddenly Daddy looked away. I knew he was looking at me. He waved to me and then went back to talking with Jesus. I awoke with a new peace in my heart, and I was never again depressed over my father's death. How great is our God!

NO GREATER LOVE

Marcia at 4 years of age.

NO GREATER LOVE

Kirby (Dad) and Martha (Mom) Malone's
Wedding Day.

NO GREATER LOVE

Kirby (Dad) and Marcia on Father's Day 1966.

NO GREATER LOVE

Jim K. and Marcia 1980.

NO GREATER LOVE

Mom K. with James and Paul (Sons) 1976.

NO GREATER LOVE

Martha (Mom) and Marcia, Christmas 1994.

NO GREATER LOVE

Jimmy and Marcia's Wedding Day 1992.

NO GREATER LOVE

Jimmy and Marcia 1993.

NO GREATER LOVE

Kathy (Forever Friend) and Marcia,
Class Reunion 1993.

NO GREATER LOVE

From Left to Right, Jerry, Grandma Van, Marcia, (Back Row) Jim, Cheryl (siblings) 1953

Chapter 5

Time with Mama

As Mama aged, she mellowed. She attended church with her neighbor, and she seemed to finally be at peace. Each time I saw her, Mama would hug me and tell me how much she loved me. She would repeatedly tell me she must have been nuts to do all the bad things she had done to me.

Almost every Saturday, I went to her flat in South St. Louis to help her with her catechism so she could join the Lutheran Church. Mama now cried when she said the blessing at meals. Her heart was uncharacteristically soft. In the past, Mama had been so full of bitterness, but somehow God had touched her heart. Possibly, she sensed her body and mind failing and knew she needed to make amends.

The night before Mama was to join the Lutheran Church, she panicked when she could not find her dental plates. She kept repeating, "Oh my Lord, oh my Lord!" as we looked for them. I helped her search

NO GREATER LOVE

in all the obvious places, but to no avail. Finally, I suggested we have a soda and regroup. When I opened the freezer door to get some ice for our drinks, I found my mother's dental plates! This was just one of many instances that signaled my mother was struggling with some type of dementia.

I did many things with Mama, taking her to doctor appointments, to the grocery store, and out to eat, but she couldn't seem to just relax during our time together. She continuously focused on what she had done to me in the past. She couldn't seem to forgive herself.

But I had forgiven Mama long ago. It did not come easily, and it was a battle that I fought for many years. At first, I didn't feel like she deserved to be forgiven because at that time she still belittled me. But eventually, because of the grace of God and His love towards me, I was able to forgive and let go of the past.

When Mama started going to church, her verbal abuse ended. Instead, she was full of remorse. Each time I walked through her door, she would hug me and cry, saying, "I have always loved you so much. I'm sorry. I'm sorry." The last time she ever told me this was on her first Mother's Day in the nursing home in 1997. She sounded so childlike as she asked, "Why are you here? I was so mean to you. I used to hate you, but now I love you." I assured Mama that I had forgiven her and that I loved her.

The next day, Mama was unable to talk plainly and could no longer be understood; her words were jumbled. She was moving into a new stage of

Alzheimer's where she was unable to communicate well. I felt like God had given me a very special gift that Mother's Day. It was the last time my mother ever told me she loved me, and she would not remember me again as her daughter.

Mama lived four more years, and my sister and I did most of the caregiving. We both worked, so we took turns running to the nursing home to check on our mother. Many nights we would go home in tears because she had sat in a wet diaper all day, or her dinner was cold and no one had fed her. Many times her glasses or hearing aids were missing. One time my mother was even dropped out of the lift because the worker was new and didn't know how to use it. Another time she was placed on the toilet and left alone, resulting in a fall. On weekends my sister and I took her out as often as we could until she wasn't able to get into the car anymore.

I remember one time in particular when I brought my mother to my home on Columbus Day. I was working for the state of Missouri at the time, and it was a holiday. I desperately needed a day off to recoup and recharge from work and from caregiving. Instead of using the day for relaxing, I decided to pick up Mama at the nursing home and bring her to my house. She loved my house and referred to it as the "dollhouse." I think that was because she loved the ballerina doll that I had gotten for Christmas in 1956 and now kept on the hearth of my fireplace.

When Mama walked through the door of my home that day, the first thing she wanted to do was to hold my doll, and then she asked if she could take it home with her. Mama napped on the couch with the doll while I prepared a pot roast with all the fixings, a dish I knew she liked. When she woke up, I said, "Mama, I cooked a nice dinner for you. After we finish our meal, I will need to take you back home."

For some reason, Mama was infuriated by that remark and angrily snapped, "If your husband was here, he wouldn't let you treat me this way." She refused to eat the meal.

My emotions got the best of me, and I answered, "You can't be mean to me anymore." I calmly sat and ate my meal while she watched me with that same look on her face that I had seen so many times when she abused me. After I finished eating, I took Mama back to the nursing home, but she wouldn't hug me or kiss me good-bye. I felt rejected all over again—just like when I was a child.

This was one of many trying times. The only thing that got me through all these emotionally draining events was my faith in God. I had to pray daily, asking God to help me show His love for Mama during the times she made me feel unloved. And He always did.

But not every encounter with Mama was bad, and I do have many fond memories. One that stands out in my mind occurred in 2001 when Jimmy and I took a seven-day cruise to celebrate our anniversary. I was so worried that my mother might forget me while I was gone. She had long ago lost her awareness of being my mother, but she did know that my siblings and I loved her. That was all that mattered. When

NO GREATER LOVE

I returned from the cruise, I walked into her room, and she was sitting in her wheelchair. When she saw me, she started laughing and clapping her hands. She could not verbalize it, but it was obvious she was glad to see me. What a wonderful memory! Mama had not forgotten me, and she gave me her usual kiss on the cheek. Sometimes it seems as though I can still feel it.

In January 2002, Jimmy and I once again took our usual anniversary cruise. My sister, brother, and I had met with staff to discuss my mother's condition. By this time, Mama was getting services from hospice, but the staff agreed my mother was stable and that I should take my trip. I told them I would be crushed if she died while I was gone, but they assured me they did not expect any change and encouraged me to go ahead with my plans. The day before I left for the cruise, I told my mother that I was going to be on vacation for a week. I also remarked, "Mom, if you decide to leave while I'm gone, I'll see Daddy and you again someday in heaven." Amazingly, she still had the strength to kiss my cheek.

Jimmy and I enjoyed our cruise. On Sunday night, the night before we were to return home, I commented to Jimmy, "I have a funny feeling in my stomach, like something is wrong with Mama." He told me I was just a worrywart and everything would be okay. When we arrived home, my sister called to tell me my mother had died just hours earlier. My heart was broken. Cheryl said, "I'm coming over right now," and she did.

When she arrived, we hugged, cried, and then went shopping for earrings for my mother to wear for her viewing at the funeral home. My mother wore my mauve wedding dress that I had worn when Jimmy and I were married in Hawaii. She also wore my pearl ring from Jim K. My mother always loved wearing dresses and jewelry, and she looked beautiful in her casket. It was a relief to know that she was now released from her pain. She had fought Alzheimer's for nine long years, and now she was free from that wicked disease.

Chapter 6

Let Freedom Ring!

Jimmy and I had always planned to live in Florida when we retired. Shortly after my mother died, Jimmy was offered a package to retire from his place of employment. We had made a pact years earlier that we would retire at the same time so we could have fun together. We had worked hard and saved for this time in our life together. I still had three years to go before I could draw my full pension, but we talked about it and decided I would take early retirement. Quite frankly, I was burned out from my job and from being a caregiver all those years with my mother. I was happy to leave my state job after working in child abuse and neglect for seventeen years. When I walked out the door on my last day, I never looked back. It was liberating!

I retired a month before Jimmy. I kept telling him he had better start clearing out his files and desk at work. My husband was a pack rat; he never threw

NO GREATER LOVE

anything away. The last week, he finally started bringing things home. He stayed at work until five on his last day, though he had been coming home early, and seemed very unsettled, as though he wasn't quite sure what to do.

A few days later in his first week of retirement, I mentioned that he needed to call his company and get our health care as retirees set up. Jimmy had always been meticulous about taking care of us. He was very logical and practical; common sense was his approach to everything. Every Saturday without fail, he would study the stock market and keep track of our assets. He was a very dependable man.

A little later, I had to remind him again to make that call to the benefits center of his employer. While he was on the phone, he asked me for his Social Security number and also our phone number. This memory lapse scared me, after having gone through Alzheimer's with my mother. I told Jimmy I thought something was wrong, and I asked him to see a doctor. He was very subdued and said he didn't think anything was wrong, but we did make a doctor's appointment.

We first saw his internist, who said he thought Jimmy had "retirement issues." I asked the doctor if he remembered my mother, and he said he did. I told him Jimmy was exhibiting many of the behaviors she had shown early in her disease. The doctor said he would order an MRI and make a referral to a neurologist. He also said he had recently put Jimmy on medication for a thyroid disorder and that this could be causing the problem with memory.

The MRI ruled out Parkinson's disease and stroke. In the meantime, I kept searching the Internet, hoping to find information that would help. I asked the neurologist to do a spinal tap on Jimmy to make sure he didn't have a brain infection. He agreed to do it because it was a possibility, but he did not think it was a likely cause for Jimmy's problems. That test, like the others, came back normal.

After being evaluated by both a neurologist and a psychologist who specialized in brain disorders, Jimmy was diagnosed with early-onset Alzheimer's. Two years later after we moved to Florida, I asked his neurologist there to check Jimmy's system for chemicals that could cause dementia-like symptoms. Jimmy had worked around dangerous chemicals in his career, and I wanted to assure myself that I was doing everything I could to look after his welfare and obtain the right diagnosis. His neurologist said that if they did find chemicals in Jimmy's system, he could be helped. But that test too came back normal.

After all the tests were completed and the diagnosis seemed sure, I reacted with anger and fear. I had just gone through more than nine years of caring for my mother with the same wicked disease, and I thought, *I can't go through this again!* I thought surely God must be playing a sick joke on me.

Initially, Jimmy was in denial about having Alzheimer's. Then he became angry. One day we were driving past the nursing home where my mother had resided, and he said, "Kill me. Please kill me so I don't have to go through what your mom did." Grief-stricken, I told him I couldn't do that and that somehow with the grace of God we would get through this together.

For the next two years, Jimmy and I were still able to have fun together. He was taking medication for memory loss, and it worked well for him. We just loved being together, and we enjoyed going to movies. We went to Cardinal baseball games, and at times it was hard to believe he was sick.

We even planned a cruise, but when we got to the port in New Orleans, Jimmy couldn't see out of one of his eyes. We saw an eye doctor there, and he told us to get back to St. Louis immediately and see a doctor who specialized in retina problems. He informed us that Jimmy had torn retinas in both eyes.

The day after we arrived home, we saw a doctor at Barnes Hospital in St. Louis. He scheduled Jimmy for surgery a day later. Unfortunately, several weeks later the retina in Jimmy's left eye detached, and he needed surgery again. Jimmy's eyesight was never the same, and he became legally blind in his left eye. Thankfully, he could still see well in his right eye.

I have often wondered if Jimmy's eye problems played a major role in the progression of his Alzheimer's. Because of his failing eyesight, Jimmy experienced so many problems with depth perception, and he often missed steps. He could no longer drive, and his limitations began to wear on him. I wanted to make all his problems go away, but I couldn't. I still feel sorrow in my heart for what he went through. It just didn't seem fair.

Jimmy and I had always planned to move to Florida when we retired. We finally decided to do it anyway, even though he was now two years into the disease. It was one of the few dreams I could make come true for him. When I asked his neurologist if the move would be okay for Jimmy, he said, "Jimmy will do fine because this is something he really wants. It's you that I worry about because you will have all the responsibility."

The doctor also cautioned me that Jimmy's disease would probably progress fast because he was young. He reminded me that Jimmy's medication would probably soon quit working, and he said if I saw a change in him, I needed to make sure I told his doctor in Florida. He was right in his predictions. Jimmy's medication did stop working just months after we arrived in Florida, so his neurologist changed medications.

Jimmy and I bought a condo in a community close to Wayne and Dottie Littlejohn, old friends from our childhood church in Illinois. Dottie, Jimmy, and I had grown up together in Full Gospel Tabernacle, and it gave me a feeling of security to know they were just around the corner from us. Without them, I doubt I would have had the courage to make the move.

Jimmy loved the ocean and beach. He jogged around the lake behind our condo, and he was so happy. But little by little, he started having problems. For example, he would soil his underwear but not tell me about it. He would just wash out the clothing and then throw it into the washing machine. I'm sure it was embarrassing for him, and I felt so sorry for him.

One night I awoke to a noise in the breakfast room. Jimmy had urinated on the wood floor, thinking the

NO GREATER LOVE

kitchen chair was the toilet. He said he knew it was wrong, but he couldn't control himself. Another time I caught him pulling his shorts down when he was outside on our front porch. I told him to pull his pants up and get into the condo before anyone saw him. He said, "I can't. My legs have mosquito bites on them, and I have to scratch them."

Another time Jimmy thought he was locked out of the condo. I was in the bathroom and didn't hear him trying to get in. The door wasn't locked, but Jimmy couldn't figure out how to open it.

Dressing Jimmy was a daily battle. He couldn't understand how to get his arm through the sleeve of his shirt. He would become so upset and get right up in my face to yell at me. Sometimes he would run out onto our lanai and yell, "Help, help, somebody help me!" At other times, he would say to me, "I hope you get Alzheimer's." I usually ended up in tears.

Most of the stress resulted from the fact that we were both overwhelmed with his disease. I wanted him to understand and help me get his arm through the sleeve. He wanted me to understand that he couldn't help himself. This is where true love and friendship kick in. You don't throw in the towel because life isn't perfect. Jimmy and I had been joined at the hip from day one in our relationship, and we had biblical values from the church we grew up in that enabled us to get through the horrors of Alzheimer's. We had a firm foundation, and it held.

I cannot stress enough the need for support from friends and family for those who are dealing with Alzheimer's. My friends, Kelly Epperson and Ruth

Okamuro, e-mailed me daily. It helped so much. Visits, phone calls, and cards were also a godsend to me. I could not have made it without all the people who truly loved Jimmy and me and showed it by their actions.

There were, of course, disappointments along the way, and at times I felt so alone. Later, after Jimmy was in assisted living, I would have to pull myself together when I went to see him so that I could boost his spirits. I would read him letters or e-mails from family and friends. He understood them, and he always grasped love.

Alzheimer's is a disease that brings out a full range of emotions from anger, fear, and pain to exhaustion, perseverance, and love. Jimmy and I hung on to each other for dear life. I didn't want him to leave me. I didn't want to let him go. I needed him. Even when he changed in appearance, I was still so drawn to him. When he held me, I still experienced a wonderful high. It was that way until the end.

But before that, while I still had him at home, I eventually grew weary and began considering adult day care for Jimmy. I talked to Jimmy about it, and we visited a few facilities, but neither of us really liked them. Jimmy felt the people there were too old, and I understood what he was saying. The thought of my husband being there upset me too. He was only fifty-nine, but most of the people in the facilities were in their seventies and eighties and very feeble. Jimmy also felt it would be degrading to have to ride a bus to the day care.

NO GREATER LOVE

Jimmy's problems were growing worse, and I was exhausted, but day care didn't seem like a good fit for him. A month later, I was so drained that I thought I just might not wake up one morning. I wondered if my caregiver role was going to put me in the grave before Jimmy.

About that time, a friend of mine from church told me of an assisted living facility for Alzheimer's patients, and she went with me to check it out. It was much nicer than the nursing home where my mother had resided. Residents had their own rooms and could go outside anytime they wanted because the facility was gated. I could take Jimmy out daily if I wanted. I liked the place and started taking him to respite there a few days each month. He enjoyed it, and I got a much-needed break.

Jimmy continued to have more problems. He just couldn't figure things out. He couldn't even remember how to shower himself. One day I was taking him to respite and he said, "You need to place me before I get worse." He knew I could never permit myself to do it, so he gave me permission. When he was placed in the assisted living facility in May 2005, he said, "Home sweet home" as we drove into the parking lot, and I felt like someone had stabbed me in the heart. His placement was the beginning stage of grieving my loss. I cried nightly for several months.

Chapter 7

The Transition

Unlike the majority of the residents, Jimmy did not fit in at assisted living. Most of the residents were much older than Jimmy, but they were still able to play bingo and engage in activities that he could not understand. Jimmy was a far cry from the man he had been all his life. He had spent twenty-nine years as a chemical engineer, but now he couldn't figure out even the smallest detail.

Jimmy and I set a routine, and it worked for us. I would come over late in the morning, and we would go out to eat and then to a movie or to the beach. Sometimes we would buy baby back ribs and bring them back to our condo for lunch. Jimmy loved those times. Had he still been living at home, I would not have been able to give him this kind of entertainment because of the exhausting daily care he now required. Our outings gave Jimmy something to look forward to on a daily basis, and I'm glad I could provide that for him.

Little by little, I had to adjust to the fact that Jimmy's body was breaking down. He started having ministrokes, and he developed severe aphasia. Our outings became extremely challenging, and my energy level was depleted most of the time.

We did, however, manage to have many good times together. We constantly made fun of ourselves. If my birthday or a holiday was coming up, I would remind Jimmy about it and tease, "What are you getting me? I'm not going to let you forget!"

Jimmy would tease back, "Diamonds, diamonds! I'll get you diamonds." True to his word, Jimmy bought me a blue sapphire and diamond ring on Valentine's Day in the year he died. It was the last ring he ever bought for me, and I was touched that he still remembered my favorite color was blue. To this day, I sometimes get hugs in the jewelry department of the store where Jimmy bought the ring; they remember my husband and how much pleasure it gave him to buy something for me.

I never took Jimmy anywhere unless I knew he would be treated respectfully. I was a thousand-pound gorilla when it came to my husband. I was very defensive of him and expected everyone to treat him with respect, and people did. The manager of Johnny Rockets would come over and kiss Jimmy on the cheek, while another employee would give him a balloon. He loved it when they danced. When we went to Perkins, Jimmy would sometimes go to the kitchen instead of the bathroom, and the waitress would come and tell me she had led him to the bathroom. At the movies, some of the young men working there learned what Jimmy liked to eat and would have it ready for us when we arrived, always treating Jimmy so special.

I myself never treated Jimmy as though he was sick. I loved him and treated him as if he was well, and we became even closer. One day as we walked down the sidewalk to the movie theater, I told him he was lucky he had me to take care of him. I then said rather petulantly, "Who will take care of me when I'm sick?"

Heartbreakingly, Jimmy sweetly answered, "I will take care of you, honey." I silently said a prayer asking God to forgive me for being so crabby. Jimmy was doing the best he could, and I wanted to always be there for him—regardless of what my future held.

On the wall in Jimmy's room, we put up Bible verses on healing. When Jimmy wanted me to read them to him, he would go over and tap his fingers on them. If he wanted me to pray with him, he simply said, "Pray." Sometimes we would just snuggle together in his twin bed.

Jimmy had told me once that sometimes he felt scared and cried at night. I assured him that we would keep praying for a miracle, but if that didn't happen, I promised to take care of him and be with him when he died. He said, "I want to die in your arms, Snugglebunny." That was his nickname for me. Years before when he had proposed to me, he had christened me Snugglebunny, and he was Snugglebear.

Our faith is what kept us glued together during all the difficult days. Right after we moved to Florida, we came home from church one day and Jimmy started crying. He said he didn't know if he was saved. I asked him, "Do you remember asking Jesus to come into your heart and forgive you of your sins?" He said he did, so I was able to reassure him that Jesus was with him and always would be. I truly do not know how we would have made it without that faith that went all the way back to our childhood.

Inevitably, Jimmy grew worse, and I decided to buy a sports car for him. That had been one of his dreams for retirement, and I wanted to fulfill it now. Jimmy was so happy and excited when he saw the car, and he promptly named it "Jimmy." It was a blue Chrysler Crossfire SRT-6, and it was a very fast car. When he wanted to go for a ride, he would say, "Let's go vroom!" After he died, I sold the car. It was just too painful to ride in it by myself. It no longer meant anything to me.

Jimmy could have been a case study in Alzheimer's; he was unique in his disease. One professional suggested he might have suffered from vascular dementia as well as Alzheimer's disease, since he kept having small strokes the last year of his life. Regardless of the cause, one thing was sure— Jimmy's brain was fried.

Besides the issues with his brain, Jimmy also struggled with eye problems, losing most of the sight in one eye. In the first year of his Alzheimer's diagnosis, he had three eye surgeries. Over time, Jimmy began having other problems as well; his body just

NO GREATER LOVE

wore out. In April 2007, he fell, and that was the beginning of the end. I could no longer take him out because he could no longer walk. The man who had set a record in high school for pole vaulting now had deteriorating muscles in his formerly rock-hard calves. He began sleeping a lot, and I knew I had lost my Jimmy.

As Jimmy's condition worsened, the assisted living facility became unable to care for him. Jimmy was dead weight now; the staff members could not continue to lift him, and the facility was not licensed to use a mechanical lift. They told me Jimmy would need to go to a nursing facility.

I was not ready for that move and begged them to keep him. I told them I would help them daily with the lifting. They said I would have to hire a private-duty attendant to come in and help get him showered and dressed for the day. I did that, but it still wasn't enough. Some attendants were good, but others neglected him or didn't even show up.

Jimmy was failing so fast. Hope Hospice became involved and sent a nurse, social worker, music therapist, and chaplain to visit Jimmy each week. Before Jimmy's aphasia kicked in, he often sang to me Willie Nelson's hit "Always on My Mind." Now the music therapist would play her guitar and sing it to us. Jimmy would weep and try to sing along with her and kiss me on the cheek.

Finally, I knew the time had come—I needed to find a nursing home for Jimmy. I quickly discovered that living in Florida is wonderful until you try to find

NO GREATER LOVE

a bed in a nursing home. I found myself hitting my head against the wall in my attempts to find a place for him. The facility that finally accepted Jimmy took pity on me as I cried on the phone with them. When I told the admissions person that he was only sixty-two, she kindly remarked, "That is my age, and I feel so bad for you."

In early August 2007, Jimmy was moved to this facility. I dreaded the day, remembering all the nursing-home problems I had experienced with my mother. I hoped that Jimmy's care would be better, since he was private pay and my mother had been on Medicaid. That hope was short lived, however, and I found it made no difference whatsoever. I was soon battling the same kind of problems that I had gone through with my mother.

One day right after Jimmy's placement, I walked into his room and discovered him on the floor with his hand under his chin and his elbow on the floor. He was able to tell me he had been like that since breakfast. His brain was unable to send the message to tell him how to take his elbow down, and he developed a nasty sore on his elbow from this incident. I was so angry at the nursing home for letting this happen, and I took pictures with my cell phone the entire day.

When I went to find help for Jimmy, the caregivers were nowhere to be found. I eventually located the nurse, who was painting a resident's fingernails, but she didn't understand the problem. She told me Jimmy kept rolling out of bed and calmly stated, "He is at risk and needs to be where he is." But I didn't buy that; Jimmy's bed could be lowered almost to the floor and the problem of his rolling off avoided. Finally, the nurse did place a paper-thin mat on the floor for Jimmy to lie on. But when he rolled off the mat, the caregivers literally dragged him back to the mat instead of using the lift.

I remember the day all this happened because it was my birthday. When I finally left the nursing home, I pounded the steering wheel of my car as I pulled out of the parking lot and said aloud, "Happy birthday, Marcia!" At midnight, when I couldn't stand it anymore, I called Hope Hospice in tears, and they seemed genuinely shocked about what had happened. They said they would send someone out to the nursing home in the morning to check it out. The hospice advocate did go to the home the next day and requested some changes be made. Jimmy was soon moved to a private room with thick mattresses on both sides of his bed.

Soon after the above incident, I was inputting the code to gain access to the dementia unit when I heard my husband moaning and groaning. When I entered the unit, I saw Jimmy all slumped down in his geriatric chair by the nurses' station. I let go on them, not realizing that the new administrator was in the next room. She came out and asked what the problem was.

I did not hesitate to show her the pictures on my cell phone from the previous incident, and I told her Jimmy was now soaked and in pain. She immediately ordered someone to find a caregiver so he could be changed. I started crying, and then Jimmy started crying. I promised him I would not let anything happen to him. I was so mad I threatened to call Nancy Grace at CNN to report their constant lack of attention to Jimmy and his needs.

The new administrator promised they would order a special padded chair that would keep Jimmy from sliding down. She kept her word, and Jimmy got the new chair, which helped quite a bit. The nursing supervisor told me that hospice didn't cover the cost of the chair, so the home bought it for him so that I would know they were trying to take good care of him. Additionally, Jimmy was put on morphine for painful muscle contractions, and it was a relief for me to see him finally at rest. He didn't seem to be in pain anymore, and that was a blessing. The week before his death, Jimmy was moved to Hope Hospice. His journey to heaven was about to begin.

Chapter 8

The Grand Finale

Ten days before Jimmy died, the staff at the nursing home informed me that he wasn't eating. I tried to give him some applesauce, but he put his hand in front of my face and emphatically said, "No!" I knew I was losing him. He was ready to go.

Jimmy had been on morphine for two months at this point. I took him outside in his chair then sat on a bench and pulled his chair close to me. I put my head on his chest and said, "Honey, I love you." Even though he was on morphine and had severe aphasia, he managed to lift his head and respond, "I love you too." He got it out, and we were both in tears.

Two days later, Jimmy was moved to Hope Hospice. I am so thankful for that because the care he received there was wonderful. The staff ministered to both Jimmy and me. He lived but one week.

On Wednesday, November 7, 2007, the night before Jimmy died, my son Paul walked into the room,

NO GREATER LOVE

and Jimmy weakly said, "Pa . . ." From that point on, Jimmy was calm. Paul kept his hand on Jimmy's chest or arm for hours, praying, reading from the Bible, and talking to him. Paul told him how important he was to him and recalled all the fun they had experienced playing tennis and racquetball together. He thanked Jimmy for being his mentor and friend.

My husband was a hero to both of my boys. I don't think I realized how much they loved their stepfather until their tributes were read at the memorial service. I was blown away by what they said. During the service for Jimmy, Paul talked about the special communication he had shared with Jimmy right up to his death. When Paul spoke to Jimmy, he could sense Jimmy's spirit talking back to him, even though Jimmy couldn't verbalize his thoughts. Jimmy felt the love Paul was giving him, and in return, Jimmy gave the love back to Paul. Paul's three daughters also called that night and told their grandpa they loved him. As they said their good-byes to him, Jimmy wept, which was really remarkable because he was severely dehydrated by this point.

On Thursday morning, November 8, 2007, the doctor came into Jimmy's room and examined him. He said because Jimmy was young and had a strong heart, he expected him to live a few more days. But something inside of me thought otherwise. I sensed an urgency to hold Jimmy; I had felt that same feeling the previous day. The nursing staff graciously allowed me to lie down with Jimmy and hold him throughout the day. They moved his catheter and positioned him so we could face each other in his small bed.

During those last two days of Jimmy's life, I held him tenderly and sang of my love for him. I also sang praise and worship songs that Jimmy knew, and sometimes I sang prayers. I just did what I felt like doing at the time. Countless times I kissed his face and told him I loved him. I held him in my arms, still savoring the magic I had experienced on our first date. I loved being with him. I always had.

From the first time we had met, Jimmy had always calmed me whenever he held me. Now I was holding him to keep my promise of being there for him when he died. I had no idea it was going to happen so fast, since the doctor had thought he would live a few more days. But I think Jimmy felt so loved by Paul and me those two last days that he was prepared and ready to go through heaven's gate.

Around ten thirty on the night my husband passed away, I told Paul to go on back to the condo to sleep, and I would call him if I needed him. I decided I was going to sleep in Jimmy's bed if the staff would allow it. God does all things well. He had a wonderful nurse on duty that night, a real angel. She said that would be fine and to just let her adjust Jimmy's catheter and move him so he would be facing me when I held him.

Another miracle happened that night. At 10:40 p.m., Snugglebunny got into bed with Snugglebear for one last snuggle. When I got into bed with my husband, he looked like his old self—my Jimmy.

When we retired in 2002, Jimmy weighed 217 pounds and was five feet nine inches tall. Now he weighed only 130 pounds and was only five feet five inches tall, but God let me see my husband as he had been rather than the little shrunken man he had become. Jimmy looked so handsome and seemed at peace.

I couldn't believe my eyes. My Jimmy was back. He seemed peaceful as I held him close. I didn't sing to him; I just snuggled up to him, enjoying the sweet intimacy of our bodies touching. It felt so good—like old times. I relaxed and closed my eyes for a few moments, just savoring the wonderful feeling of holding Jimmy in my arms.

Finally, I opened my eyes and looked at Jimmy. I rubbed his head, kissed him on his forehead, and told him I loved him. Then I put my hand on his chest and said, "Jesus, Jesus, Jesus." On the third "Jesus," I felt my husband's spirit leave. He simply flew away. It was like the wisp of a butterfly's wings, a mere flutter and gentle breeze. It was faster than I could blink an eye. I still marvel at that night.

I kept moving my hand all over Jimmy's chest. I was stunned! I just closed my eyes and relished this moment with my heavenly Father. I did not want to lose this feeling of being in the presence of a holy God. It felt like the Lord had taken a scrub brush and washed me clean; it was wonderful.

I looked at the clock, and it was 11:00 p.m. I got out of bed and found one of the nurses. We went back to Jimmy's room, and she confirmed his death. I went down to the chapel and called Paul while the staff prepared Jimmy for our viewing. Paul had just

NO GREATER LOVE

walked into the condo when I called and said he would come right back. I made a few other calls, and then Paul arrived.

The nurse took us back to Jimmy's room. They had placed a beautiful quilt on him. There was a table at the end of his bed with a lit candle, fresh flowers, family pictures, and the Bible opened to Psalm 23. Paul said, "Mom, he's really gone. I can't feel his spirit like I did earlier. I've always believed in heaven, but I really do now. He's gone. He's free. He's not here." Paul and I had spent so much time loving Jimmy and praying with him the past two days that we didn't stay long. What was in the bed was Jimmy's earthly shell. Our Jimmy was gone.

As Paul and I drove home, he commented, "Mom, I feel like running down the beach and shouting, 'He's free! He's free!' " We were both so overjoyed that Jimmy was now free of pain. When we got home, we were too hyper to sleep, so we stayed up and talked about our lives with Jimmy.

After Paul flew back to Missouri, it felt strange to be alone. Even though I knew that Jimmy was finally at rest after all the years of sickness, it was hard to accept that he was really gone. My sister, Cheryl, flew down and assisted me with so many things and helped me through a difficult time. After she left, my son James came down and spent Thanksgiving with me. He helped me write Jimmy's obituary, and he also created the program for Jimmy's memorial service that I wanted to have at the church we had grown up in (Jimmy had been cremated). Jimmy and I had first met in the primary department of our

NO GREATER LOVE

Illinois church when we were ten years old, so it seemed like a fitting location.

The holidays were quickly approaching, so after prayer and much thought, I decided to hold the memorial service on January 2, 2008, our sixteenth wedding anniversary. When Jimmy first got sick, we talked about what kind of service he would like, and he had said, "Tell them our love story." Jimmy's death had been so special that I felt I should talk about the last two days of his life, yet I also wanted to honor his wishes and share how we had fallen in love. When I prayed about what I should say, I sensed God saying, "The last two days of Jimmy's life is your love story."

On December 31, 2007, I flew back to St. Louis for the memorial service. My brother, Jerry, and his wife, Jerri, and Cheryl and her husband, Mike, picked me up at the airport, and we went back to my sister's house in Godfrey, Illinois. The next day my older brother, Jim, came over, and it felt so good to be with all my siblings.

Later that evening, however, I hit the panic button. I thought, *What am I doing? Why did I think I could give Jimmy's eulogy?* Seeing my anxiety, Cheryl said, "You need to call Paul."

I took her advice, and Paul helped me to calm down. "Now, Mom, why did you tell me you wanted to have this service?" he prodded.

"I don't know!" I wailed.

"Yes, you do," he patiently answered. "You said you wanted to honor Jimmy and God and to tell everyone what happened the night Jimmy died so people would have hope."

His calm demeanor and soothing words worked their magic. Taking a deep breath, I sighed. "Yes, you are right. I feel better now."

Paul said a prayer over the phone, and I went to bed with the assurance I was doing the right thing.

The next day, the service went well. I felt God's Spirit as I spoke of our love story and as my boys honored Jimmy with words of honor and respect. I was able to have closure and say good-bye to my Jimmy. It was very special to have the service at Grace Church (formerly known as Full Gospel Tabernacle) in Fairview Heights, Illinois, where Jimmy and I had learned our values and accepted Christ. Paul and I both sensed God's Spirit with us as we talked about our love for Jimmy and honored him for the man he was.

Chapter 9

What Do I Do Now?

When I returned to Florida after Jimmy's memorial service, I was physically exhausted. My knees and legs had been damaged from all the lifting I had done with Jimmy and my mother, and I started having problems with them. I have never felt so wrung out as I did then. The last fifteen years had been spent taking care of first my mother and then my husband, and now my body was reacting to the trauma inflicted upon it.

I also went through leadership training for a new grief-share class at my church, and I attended the thirteen-week class for my own loss. During that quiet time of resting and healing, I began writing this book.

In April 2007, a few weeks before Jimmy fell, God made it real to me that I was to show His love, mercy, and grace during my husband's illness in order to demonstrate to others who He is. Little did I know at the time that Jimmy's health was about to

NO GREATER LOVE

change, and I certainly had no idea what God was going to do the night Jimmy died.

But from that point in April onward, I drew closer to God. I felt very humble, and I reached a point where I was compelled to kneel in prayer at my bed nightly. With a new reverence for Him burning in my heart, I could no longer pray lying in bed. I felt like falling on my face before my magnificent God. Looking back, I know He was preparing my heart for what lay ahead, but at the time, of course, I did not know that.

If you are in a crisis situation or someone you love is sick or dying, always remember that there is hope. I do not know how anyone can go through life's difficult times without God. I am so thankful that I grew up in a church that taught me to call upon the name of the Lord. I had heard all my life that there is power in Jesus' name, and I did believe it; however, I had never really experienced that power in action like I did when I said "Jesus" and felt Jimmy's spirit leave so quickly. It was an awesome experience that has changed my life forever.

I'm so thankful the Lord gave me such sweet physical closeness with Jimmy his last two days of life. It was a very special time to say good-bye. I'm also glad Paul was there to share in the miracle of Jimmy's entrance into heaven. Because of those two special, spiritual days, God placed a dream inside of me to bring encouragement, comfort, and hope to others who are going through similar circumstances.

My desire was soon granted a few weeks after Jimmy passed away. I was in a restaurant in the St.

NO GREATER LOVE

Louis airport, and a man was sitting across from me. He politely asked if I lived in St. Louis. I responded that I was from Florida and that my husband had recently died. He quickly answered, "Oh, I'm sorry."

I said, "No, don't be," and then I shared about Jimmy and how he had died. The man listened intently and then somberly replied, "I needed to hear this. I can't wait to tell my wife. My mother has Alzheimer's, and I'm struggling with all of it. Promise me you'll put this in writing so people will know they can have hope."

God continues to bring so many people across my path that need to hear this message of hope. Because we are mortal, even we Christians sometimes struggle with death and the process of dying. Since the night Jimmy died, however, I have gained an entirely different perspective on death, and now I see it in a new light. Death is nothing for the Christian to fear, but rather it is to be celebrated! O death, where is thy sting?

Romans 8:28 states, "And we know that all that happens to us is working for our good if we love God and are fitting into his plans. God has it all under control, and we can rest in His love. Psalm 17:15 says, "But as for me, my contentment is not in wealth but in seeing you and knowing all is well between us. And when I awake in heaven, I will be fully satisfied, for I will see you face to face." There is no fear in death. He will safely take us home.

Conclusion

On April 19, 2008, I said my final good-bye to Jimmy. Two of my friends, Amy Bergez and Alan Feckanin, took me out in Alan's boat to release Jimmy's remains in the Gulf of Mexico. We went to a beautiful place between Pine Island and Gasparilla Island. The weather was perfect, the water was calm, and it seemed like heaven was smiling down upon us. When I got ready to release Jimmy's ashes into the ocean, Amy and I first tossed rose petals into the water. I then said good-bye and lovingly placed my husband's ashes into the water.

Jimmy's favorite bird was the pelican. From the time we got into the boat until we reached our destination for the ceremony, an abundance of pelicans flew above us. I thought it very fitting for this beautiful occasion.

Jimmy also loved dolphins. Once in a while, we would see them when we were at the beach, but they were usually too far away for us to see them very well. But God in all His glory allowed the dolphins to visit us for this special event of placing Jimmy's ashes into the water. Dolphins were swimming and bobbing up and down all around us, and one in particular flipped on his back twice and waved his tail at us. I thought, *If this gets any better, I don't know what I'll do!* Through the pelicans and the dolphins, God was showering me with His love in a way that was special to Jimmy and me.

As Jimmy's remains drifted away, the rose petals followed along. We slowly sailed away as the ashes made their home in the briny deep. I knew that a new day awaited me and that God's plan would unfold.

Epilogue

In June 2008, I decided to spend the summer in Missouri near my children and grandchildren. As my son James and I traveled through the various states on our way back to Missouri, I felt so lost. The farther away we were from Florida, the more anxiety I experienced. I finally broke down and sobbed, "I want to go back to Florida." I missed Jimmy so much, and I wanted to be near the ocean that contained his ashes. James did his best to console me as we continued our trip.

Soon we pulled up to a convenience store, and I got out to buy a soda. When I got back into the car, I noticed a funny-looking coin mixed in with my change. Astounded, I turned to James and said, "You're not going to believe this!" As he glanced at me, I showed him a Finnish coin.

Jimmy's love for Finland was well known. In fact, James had mentioned it in his tribute at Jimmy's memorial service. When Jimmy worked in Finland in 2001, he sent me a series of love poems. He loved

NO GREATER LOVE

everything about Finland and had often said he wished he could live there. Shortly before he became ill, he took a trip to Finland and rode a snowmobile. It was thirty below zero, and he had to wear protective clothing, but Jimmy had a blast riding through the woods at night.

Now what are the odds that I would receive a Finnish coin in Kentucky? But that is exactly what happened. We left the convenience store and rode for five more hours; by this time we were in Missouri. I felt tearful again, as we stopped to get another snack. Walking into the store, I was immediately confronted with a sign that read, "Fear not, for I am with thee!" I knew these words, coupled with the Finnish coin, were gifts from God. Some would call them "winks" from God, little reminders that He was with me. The Finnish coin allowed me to feel close to Jimmy once again, and the sign reminded me that I wasn't alone and that God's presence would continue to be with me. God has a plan for all of us, and He assured me of that fact on a day when I needed it so badly.

Thoughts about Grief

When Jimmy died, I assumed that the bulk of my grieving was behind me. I had been grieving for years in my journey through Alzheimer's with him. By the time he died, he had been out of our home for over two years. I thought I had already grieved his loss and that now it was time to move on in my life. But what a rude awakening awaited me!

The longer Jimmy was gone, the more I missed him. Even though I had experienced such a wonderful miraculous event when he left this earth, an experience for which I felt truly blessed and chosen, I still had a measure of pain to work through. At first, I couldn't understand why I was struggling with Jimmy's death after being with him when he walked through heaven's gates. After all, I had had years of pain and grieving. Shouldn't I just feel relief? I did feel relief, but after many months, I realized I still had not completed the grieving process. I had to come down to earth and walk through my grief.

I let God know I wasn't happy about this stage of mourning.

I spent the summer of 2008 in physical pain from the wear and tear on my back and legs from caring for my husband. As I went through months of hardly being able to walk or ride in a car, I kept saying to God, "This is so unfair. I took care of my mother and husband for fifteen years, and I deserve a break." Nonetheless, I suffered for months. Though I am much better now, I'm still recovering.

During these months, I cried out to God in anguish. But the more I prayed, the more grief I seemed to feel. God finally got through to me and showed me that grief is a process, and I needed to grieve for my husband. To do so took nothing away from my last few glorious moments with him.

Going through the grief process cleansed me and created a heart of empathy for others. I needed to walk through this valley so I could move on in my life. I was so spiritually high the night my husband died, and I knew that I was to share that experience to give people hope. But there was another side of the story that needed to be told. God let me know that I also needed to tell about the time in the valley that so often follows the time on the mountaintop.

Today I reminisce and remember the good times I had with Jimmy. When the tears come, I don't stop them. I am truly allowing myself to feel the pain of the loss. As I finish this book, I still miss Jimmy. I'm not sure the pain has lessened; it still hurts. I see couples all around me and think, *That should be us*. However, when I stay focused on the glorious night my husband joined Jesus in heaven, I know there is *no greater love*, and I feel healed and ready to share that love with others.

A NEW BEGINNING

On February 5, 2010, I had the pleasure of meeting our women's pastor, Connie Weisel, and attending First Assembly of God's Women's Retreat on Sanibel Island. This event was life changing for me.

I quietly wept the entire service on the first night of the retreat. I felt like a vial of oil was being poured over me. God healed me in so many ways during this experience. His still voice spoke to me in the middle of the night that it was a new beginning......a new start. When I was prayed for on Saturday morning, I felt a release of joy within me. I felt renewed in my spirit. The heaviness of grief I had carried for so long had lifted.

On Saturday evening the speaker talked about the fear of the unknown. I could relate and said to myself, "Oh God, don't let me make any mistakes at this time of my life. Take away any fear I have over my future." I can't begin to tell you what happened inside of me that night, but I have never surrendered myself so fully to God. It was a night of repentance and restoration for me.

Sunday morning the emphasis was on missions and heeding the call of God. As Pastor Connie prayed for me, I felt a newness of life in my heart. I am on my way back to wherever God wants to take me. It's been a process for the last three years and started shortly before my husband died. The Lord is bringing me into a new dimension of who He is in my life.

I am so thankful I was able to share my experiences with you in this book. We are all chosen by God to serve. His love and forgiveness is never ending. I pray God's richest blessings upon you.

Tips for Caregivers, Friends, and Families

Caregivers:

1. Take time for *you!* You can burn out quickly if you don't get much-needed breaks.
2. Get involved in a support group or church group, or see a counselor to help you through the rough times.
3. Tell people if you need help. My church was an excellent resource for me. Don't be shy. Create a good support system.
4. Learn to spoil yourself. I treated myself to a massage or manicure and pedicure. I had never done these things until Jimmy got sick, and it helped a lot. I took a day off from time to time to have a "me" day.
5. Stay in touch with people. I had to push myself to participate in events at church and other places and tended to shy away from people at times. But I always felt better after

NO GREATER LOVE

    I made myself attend a supper at church or some other event.
6. Don't feel guilty when you need to place your loved one in a facility. I beat myself up with guilt over Jimmy's placement, but it was the only option I had. My sweet husband told me to place him, taking the responsibility from me because he knew I wouldn't do it.
7. Find something to laugh about daily when spending time with your loved one. I took Jimmy out daily when he was at assisted living. Although he suffered from aphasia and it was difficult to have a conversation with him, we somehow managed to communicate. We laughed a lot, even if it was about us! Laughter is good for the soul.
8. No matter how ill my husband became, he understood the language of love. Showing affection to him was important for both of us. He knew who loved him and who didn't. Hospice assured me that he would understand everything anyone said to him until he died, even though he might not acknowledge it. I showered him with love the week he lived at Hope Hospice and I'm so glad I did.

Friends and Families:

1. Stay in touch with the caregiver and sick person, even if it's a two-line e-mail saying, "I'm thinking of you." My husband knew until the end who called and stayed in touch and

who didn't. He had his heart broken at times. Don't assume the sick person won't know the difference because he or she has a memory problem. Not all Alzheimer's patients forget their family and friends. Jimmy remembered them until the end.

2. Don't tell the caregiver and ill person that you will be back in a certain time period and then not do it. It's very hurtful. Most of us have good intentions, but life has a way of distracting us from keeping our commitments. Rather than promise, "I'll see you in a few weeks," say, "I will be back as soon as I can, but I am not sure at this point when that will be." That way there is no letdown for the person fighting the disease or for the caregiver.

3. Do invite the caregiver to dinner or a social event. I remember once going to our clubhouse to pick up a carryout dinner rather than cooking a meal. I ran into a friend there who casually remarked, "Oh, eating in tonight?" I wanted to snap back, "Yes, I'm eating in because no one asked me out. Enjoy your meal with your husband!" Of course, she didn't mean to hurt me by her remark, and I'm not saying my attitude was right, but my point is, it's important to remember the caregiver.

4. Do not forget to pray for the caregiver.

If you would like to contact Marcia, her e-mail address is: marcia45@embarqmail.com.

OLD COUPLE WALKS THE BEACH

A man and his wife like to walk the Beach,
Peace and tranquility to beseech
Their skin turns gold as they grow old,
Because they love to walk the beach.

The beach is a picture of life,
Of living and dying and strife,
Maybe that is why, before they should die,
They love to walk the beach.

The waves like to visit the beach,
Some days they must have long reach,
They bring in fresh shells and stories to tell,
Of the ways of hard life in the seas.

In the evening the sun is still warm,
But the ultraviolet will do no harm,
So the couple is safe to be in this place,
While they finish the day arm in arm.

Their love is endless like the sea,
Because that's the way it was meant to be.

Written by Jimmy Jones in Finland on 1/28/2001